Stop selling. Start attracting.

The selling phase of your life and business is now over. Discover how to **Always Be The Buyer**.

Knowing Who You'll Always Be

Knowing Where You're Going

**Knowing What
You're Leaving**

**Knowing What
Matters Most**

**Knowing What
Doesn't Matter**

**Knowing Who
Will Grow**

**Knowing Why
They'll Stay**

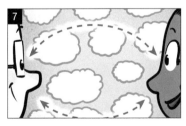

**Knowing What
Growers Want**

Six Ways To Enjoy This Strategic Coach Book

Text **60 Minutes**	The length of our small books is based on the time in the air of a flight between Toronto and Chicago. Start reading as you take off and finish the book by the time you land. Just the right length for the 21st-century reader.
Cartoons **30 Minutes**	You can also gain a complete overview of the ideas in this book by looking at the cartoons and reading the captions. We find the cartoons have made our Strategic Coach concepts accessible to readers as young as eight years old.
Audio **120 Minutes**	The audio recording that accompanies this book is not just a recitation of the printed words but an in-depth commentary that expands each chapter's mindset into new dimensions. Download the audio at **strategiccoach.com/go/ABTB**
Video **30 Minutes**	Our video interviews about the concepts in the book deepen your understanding of the mindsets. If you combine text, cartoons, audio, and video, your understanding of the ideas will be 10x greater than you would gain from reading only. Watch the videos at **strategiccoach.com/go/ABTB**
Scorecard **10 Minutes**	Score your Buyer Mindset at **strategiccoach.com/go/ABTB**. First, score yourself on where you are now, and then fill in where you want to be a year from now.
ebook **1 Minute**	After absorbing the fundamental ideas of the Always Be The Buyer concept, you can quickly and easily share them by sending the ebook version to as many other individuals as you desire. Direct them to **strategiccoach.com/go/ABTB**

Thanks to the Creative Team:

Adam Morrison

Kerri Morrison

Hamish MacDonald

Shannon Waller

Jennifer Bhatthal

Victor Lam

Margaux Yiu

Christine Nishino

Willard Bond

Peggy Lam

Always Be The Buyer

Every entrepreneur starts out as a great salesperson. It's how you built and grew your business. But at a certain point, you're creating so much value that you become sought-after in the marketplace. And that's when you become the buyer. No longer will you take just any opportunity that comes your way. No longer will just any customer or client be worth your time and effort.

Discover the characteristics of a buyer mindset that attracts others to you, and leave the selling phase of your life behind.

Contents

Introduction   10
Everyone Wants To Join You

Chapter 1   16
Knowing Who You'll Always Be

Chapter 2   22
Knowing Where You're Going

Chapter 3   28
Knowing What You're Leaving

Chapter 4   34
Knowing What Matters Most

Chapter 5   40
Knowing What Doesn't Matter

Chapter 6   46
Knowing Who Will Grow

Chapter 7   52
Knowing What Growers Want

Chapter 8   58
Knowing Why They'll Stay

Conclusion   64
Buyers Multiplying More Buyers

The Strategic Coach Program   70
For Ambitious, Collaborative Entrepreneurs

Introduction
Everyone Wants To Join You

You permanently occupy the center of everyone else's interests and aspirations because they want to participate in and contribute to the innovative ways you're uniquely transforming your life and the world around you.

Competition for status is often a strong element of a person's life.

Competing to be more successful than everyone else—in areas including what we consume, what we can do, and who we know—is a crucial part of how so many people make their way in life.

The factors that determine status all tend to be things that we acquire outside of ourselves, so during the time of your life that you're focused on competing for status, you're not necessarily focusing on improving things inside of yourself.

Everybody's selling—you're not.

What if instead of competing like everyone else, you kept developing within yourself a value that's uniquely yours? Instead of selling yourself to other people, other people will be drawn to join you because they admire you. This is the next stage. Competing and selling got you to where you are, but the selling period of your life is now over.

In this stage, you stick to working on yourself, exploring and expanding your own uniqueness in such a way that other people find you admirable and aspire to achieve a personal uniqueness, as you've done.

From now on, you're going to attract the increasingly transformative capabilities and resources of other individuals into your biggest and best endeavors, and your main activity is never going to be to sell.

A seller is someone who can get rejected. A buyer is the one who does the rejecting. A buyer knows exactly what and who they're looking for. You want to be in a position where you're the one choosing whether an opportunity or relationship fits. You want to be the one who sets the standards.

Simply being more of who you are.

All of your best thinking, decision making, innovations, achievements, and results can now be entirely focused on expanding who you've already become.

This is what other people most want to learn from you. Everyone would rather figure out how to be increasingly who they really are than twist themselves out of shape trying to be someone else.

We all take inspiration from other people, but we still want to be ourselves. We can't become the people that inspire us.

Revolving around your center.

You're going to notice how different your life is from the vast majority of the outwardly talented and successful people you encounter.

Those people always feel anxious that what they most need is outside of themselves and their experiences, whereas you feel totally confident that your entire future is simply a matter of reinforcing who you already are at your center.

It's a loop because part of our intelligence is how we think about our own personal experience, and part of it is the social proof of other people finding that what we discover about ourselves is also valuable in helping them discover things about themselves.

If you operate from the outside in, everyone else is in competition with you. But if you focus on who you really are, operating from the inside out, people will find value in you without your having to recreate who you are.

You'll also find resonance with people who might be doing something entirely different than you are but who are operating in the same sort of way.

Everything's changing—you're not.
In a world where the loudest messages are about how everything is unpredictably changing, you're going to have the daily experience that everything that's important to you is becoming predictably more purposeful and powerful.

I can see a direct connection between myself at age seventy-five and myself at age six. My fascination and motivation are not very different. I'm the same person now, just with a lot more capability and experience.

The present you is always better than the previous you, and the future you is always better than the present you. Compare yourself to no one except who you used to be and who you want to be.

Other people might tell you that they find it useful to make outside comparisons, but in reality, the moment you go outside and start comparing yourself to how other people appear to you, the magic is broken.

Life accelerates—you're slowing down.

Other people are always showing up in new ways—from the clothes they're wearing to the restaurants where they eat. If you compare yourself to others and try to keep up with them, it will seem that life is speeding up and even bypassing you.

But you're unique, and you can't be unique and be like everyone else. You have to make a choice to do one or the other: either be yourself and work on expanding your uniqueness, or compare your knowledge of yourself on the inside to what someone else is projecting on the outside.

You'll notice increasing complaints from those around you that "life is speeding up," but this won't be your experience at all. In fact, it will be just the opposite for you: everything about your personal life will seem to slow down.

This will multiply your attractiveness and value to talented, successful, and ambitious achievers who want to establish the same quality of living at the center of their own lives. You'll no longer have to think about selling, but only about being more and more the kind of person that other people want to work with and collaborate with.

An important difference between being a buyer and a seller is your mentality. In the following chapters, I'll discuss the characteristics of a buyer mindset and the key things a buyer has to know.

Chapter 1
Knowing Who You'll Always Be

You derive maximum value from your best and worst experiences to determine who you always are when you're at your best.

One of our central human abilities is to recognize and distinguish between what we like and what we don't like—and it's important to take those feelings seriously.

From the time we're children, we're reinforcing our likes and dislikes. This distinction has always been among the most valuable to me in categorizing my various life experiences.

It's also important to own your experience and never blame it on anything outside of yourself, because your experience doesn't happen outside of yourself. Your experience is what you choose to make it mean.

Owning who you've been.

Your greatest strength for the future lies in first taking total ownership of everything you've done in your past so that all of it can be a source of new knowledge and skills going forward.

It can be hard for some people to take responsibility for their experiences because it's easy to blame others when things go wrong. In fact, some people are more driven by failure than by success because they're actually motivated by blaming, and failure gives them a lot more opportunity to blame. But blaming is not taking responsibility for your experiences.

Your own experience is really the only experience you have full access to. Your ability to understand other people and their lives is directly proportional to how much of your own experience you've taken responsibility for.

Learning from worst to best.

All of your past experiences in which you've failed or experienced setbacks can be of greater value to you in the future because each of the negative results taught you how to achieve and appreciate positive results.

If you're shielded from failure, you're deprived of knowing what success is. You need to have negative experiences against which you can judge and fully appreciate positive experiences.

Usually, we experience failures because there's a fault in our approach, and at a certain point, we'll figure out whether it's the fault of something outside of ourselves, something inside of ourselves, or, as is usually the case, a combination of both.

It's important to have a creative response to every type of experience you have so you can learn what went right from positive experiences and how to prevent negative experiences from reoccurring.

Growing from integrity outward.

When you tell the truth about all of your past results, you'll be amazingly rewarded because each time you understand how they can support your future growth, you'll feel that every aspect of who you are is based on a solid foundation.

It's easier to tell yourself the truth about your failures than about your successes because while your successes are celebrated outside of yourself, you're generally alone with your failures. People usually don't want to be with you with your failures, which means that you won't be confused by other people's input. The experiences are all yours, and you'll become skillful at dealing with your failures.

Some version of everything you experience in life has happened to other people, but there's uniqueness to how you personally experience it and deal with it. And as you get better at dealing with failures, you can become useful at helping others deal with their own.

We're not usually given encouragement to deal with the negative aspects of our experiences, but when you can take a negative experience and learn a lesson from it that you can apply positively to the future, you're transforming the negative experience.

And you can give yourself credit for trying what led to the negative experience in the first place while you move forward confidently with the lesson you've learned.

Consistently simple.
The focused activity of identifying, examining, and then transforming your negative and positive experiences into new knowledge and capability for the future will deepen and multiply a uniquely consistent confidence in all your new experiences.

In my own life, I've found that the more I transform my experiences, the more confident I feel that I'll be able to deal with anything new, negative, or jarring in the future. Something may throw me off for an hour or for a day, but I have enough practice of transforming my experience that I have the confidence I'll be able to do it again.

It's your job to transform your experiences, nobody else's. And in order to take 100 percent responsibility, you have to eliminate all blaming. Blaming overflows into your relationship with the outside world, and people who blame are not highly desirable.

Doing anything other than taking full ownership of your experience means that you're putting the blame on outside factors, and no learning can come from that.

Others are attracted to who you are.

You'll find that the more you expand your internal trans-formation of unique experiences into intentional learning, the more that other self-transforming individuals will be attracted to you.

There are other individuals who will be interested in this way of owning and transforming experiences, and it's important that it's reinforced by people like you who are doing the same thing.

Much of the world isn't operating this way, and if you're doing it alone, without a community, it takes a lot of energy. It's like you're going against gravity.

This path is not about rugged individualism. You have to always be starting at your center and moving outward. When you connect with others who are operating using the same process, you reinforce it for one another, and mutual transformation happens.

Chapter 2
Knowing Where You're Going
You continually clarify your best possible future with measurable goals that represent the best growth of your best capabilities.

Goals are a picture of yourself in the future, and you can only have this picture of yourself as a function of where you used to be.

You have a transformational growth path behind you and the developmental ability to review your experiences, and you also have a future capability.

You're comparing backwards, and now you can see a vision of a future version of yourself. You see where you're truly enjoying yourself right now, and you can see where it could be even more enjoyable. You can attach it to certain events and achievements in the future.

That's how you know where you want to go next.

Measurably growing your best future.
It's important to always see ahead and plan your next achievements in the form of measurable growth.

There are only two ways you can measure: by a number, which can be an amount of money earned or a date that something is to take place by, or an event. Either way, it will be clear in the end whether you were successful in achieving your goal because either the number will have been reached or it won't have, or the event will have taken place or it won't have.

Using concrete measurements that are distinctly either achieved or not is key. Having a vague goal like "I want this to be better" won't let you know for sure if you were truly successful in achieving it.

No matter how much work you've done on something, until the number is reached or the event happens, you're still in the project. The future doesn't exist until the measurement is true.

Bypassing all the "in groups."

A lot of people's progress is measured by the approval of a group of which they're a member. These groups could be peers, family members, colleagues, communities. And it's the group's say-so whether they're doing things right. People in this situation don't use any internal measurement to know for themselves how much progress they're making.

But your internally driven ambition enables you to achieve and accomplish in ways that bypass those conventional "in groups" whose approval and permission might slow down or stop the initiatives of individuals who aren't as internally driven as you are.

"In groups" are status-driven, not transformative. But status isn't one of the measurements we can use to determine real progress.

People who are transformatively connected to each other aren't part of an "in group." They just consider one another to be people it's great to be around. They cooperate and collaborate with one another, which has no status value but tremendous capability value and transformative value.

Internally governed and directed.

When the way forward is governed and directed by your own self-created laws and rules, you can make your way ahead in the world independently. That's what autonomy means.

Every time you transform an experience, there's a law for the future that comes out of it—always do that again in similar situations in the future, or never do that again. We're constantly making laws from our own experience.

This is because we try to avoid going through unpleasant experiences more than once. If you have a painful experience, your brain will hold onto it and it will continue to pain you until you get the lesson from the experience and learn how to avoid it in the future.

The toughest thing about a negative experience is determining what worked about it. It takes real courage to find the value in a situation even when things don't go as planned. Then think back and identify everything about the situation that bothered you. When you've determined both what worked and what didn't work, you can create a list of the things to remember when you find yourself in a similar situation in the future.

Anytime you go through this process, you transform a negative experience and create new laws for yourself moving forward.

Enjoying others' unpredictability.

Being directed by the laws you make will also allow you to best take advantage of outside resources.

You'll always be open to the variety and unpredictability of other people's ideas, skills, and initiatives because whether any of them are useful to you is determined by the value they add to your internally generated initiatives.

You can avoid making a mistake that someone else has made by learning from their experience. If someone tells you about a situation they were in and what they figured out from it, that can save you an enormous amount of time.

So if I trust that someone else is good at transforming their negative experiences into breakthroughs, I'm all ears. It's interesting and useful information that I can apply to my own future situations.

Moving when others are stuck.

Almost every economic activity in the world comes out of someone learning to solve a problem that paralyzes other people. It can be much easier to get clear on other people's problems than your own because you're less likely to be emotionally paralyzed by other people's problems.

When it comes to someone else's problem, you can have clarity and figure out if there's anything from your own experience that can be of use in this other person's situation.

When you make use of your original thinking and enterprise, you can make remarkable, independent progress everywhere you choose at times when others who aren't original or independent are stopped and stuck by their lack of initiative.

We can be of enormous use to each other if we're first of all of enormous use to ourselves.

Chapter 3
Knowing What You're Leaving
You increasingly transform your daily experience going forward to eliminate everything that doesn't support who you're growing into.

Once you've transformed the raw material of a past experience into future usefulness, there's no reason to go back to the experience again.

Our experience includes a lot of content, and the lessons from it are the context that you get from that content. It doesn't come with the lesson included. You have to create the lesson.

If someone has a lot of experience but never transforms it into lessons, eventually they won't have room for anything new because the content without context keeps building up.

Maximizing your past.
As much time as we might spend thinking about our future and our past, we don't spend a single second of time in either. We exist only in the present.

But the greatest capability you have in the present involves both your past and your future: it's extracting maximum value from your past experiences as an expanding foundation of greater performance and results in the future.

Some people have a tendency to take positive experiences for granted and to shove negative experiences in a box, never to be thought of again.

But if you want to experience positive feelings you've had again, and you'd rather avoid repeating negative experiences, you can't take any experience, positive or negative, for granted, or try to avoid thinking about it. It's all there to be transformed.

Experience is raw material.
You can't go back and relive the past, but you can visualize what happened and create new lessons out of it.

Nothing gets created out of nothing; you have to start with something. And experience is what we have to create lessons out of.

And so everything that's ever happened to you can be considered simply as raw material you can use to have bigger and better experiences going forward.

I've discovered that when something very emotional happens to me, it stays with me until I've converted it into lessons. Before I knew this was the case, I could become paralyzed by negative experiences for long periods of time.

Then I figured out that I have to first of all say, "What do I want this experience to mean to me?" And I have to tell myself, "It's not the experience itself; it's what I want it to mean."

I have to take responsibility and then put a purpose to it. That's how I get unlocked from the experience and move forward.

Learning equals winning.
Everything you can remember has the potential to expand your ability to learn something new and powerful in all of

your future circumstances. It doesn't matter how painful an experience was. If you learn from it, it's a win. And the pain goes away.

While you're in a painful situation, you might find yourself saying, "I'll never get over this." But if you transform the experience into a lesson, you can get over it more quickly. And the painful experience won't repeat itself.

Winning is great, learning is important—and while winning isn't necessarily always learning, learning is always winning.

The only time you're truly losing is when you're not winning *or* learning.

Liking who you've been.

If you're always transforming your past experiences into lessons, there's no way you'll ever be embarrassed about who you were in the past.

The only kind of experience you could be embarrassed about is one where you're not learning, but instead blaming some outside factor for how you feel inside.

If you're always trying to get away from who you've been, you won't be transforming your past into a better future.

You want to always be growing into a bigger and better version of yourself, which means that you're always ahead of where you were in the past.

As you constantly use lessons from your past experiences in order to grow in the present and create your own future, you can like and admire who you used to be and who you've been all along. Liking and admiring yourself for your creative mindset can expand your ability to like and admire the same quality in other people.

It's all your property.
No one can impose their own meaning onto an experience of yours. You're the only person who has any say over what each and every one of your experiences can mean over the course of your entire lifetime.

You can ask people what their experiences mean to them, but you can never tell anyone what their experience means. And if you assume you know what another person's experience means to them, there's every chance you're wrong, because it's subjective.

You have the experiences, you find the meaning in them, and you create the lessons out of them that you then use for yourself as you move forward.

Also, consider that creatively making use of your past can have an effect on how you experience things in the present.

Since, as you go along, you're recognizing that every time you take responsibility for a past experience, you're getting value out of it, you'll realize that you have a chance in the present to take more responsibility for experiences that are happening right now.

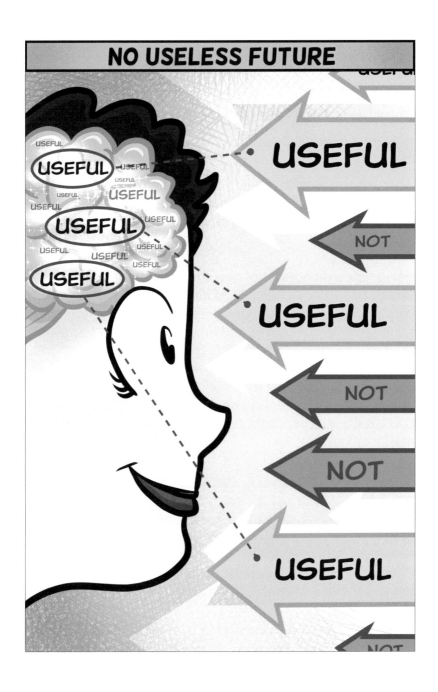

Chapter 4
Knowing What Matters Most
You create powerful filters of high personal standards by which you determine which ongoing experiences are best for growth.

If you've made good use of your prior experience, it's made you more knowledgeable about what you're really good at and what's really interesting to you.

And even more importantly, it's given you a very clear line going forward about what new experiences, relationships, opportunities, and possibilities are going to be useful to you. The strongest of those will be in the category of relationships—what relationships do you really want to have?

The biggest understanding and capability you gain from transforming your past experiences into lessons is being able to define your standards. You know what's acceptable and what's unacceptable, and this knowledge is what matters most.

Filtering out useless experiences.
When you're aware of the value of your past experiences, you can avoid repeating any experiences you've already determined are no longer useful to you. You'll encounter future situations where you'll immediately be able to say, "This is too much like a negative experience I had, and I'm not doing that again."

You'll maximize the value of your past for the future, and you can become more and more skillful at doing that.

For example, in the past, I got into situations where it took me months to discover that a relationship I was in just wasn't good for me. Now, I can simply spend some time listening to how someone talks about themselves and about their other relationships, and determine right away if it would be a bad relationship for me to enter into.

Saving that time and stress is a result of my creating useful lessons from the negative experiences I've had in the past.

Meeting your best standards.

When you have a "buyer mindset," you continually use your best learning from all of your experiences to create standards about what will be useful to your future and what won't be. You always want to be upgrading your present based on the best standards you've created.

There are always a lot of possibilities, and you have a bigger and better future plan, and that's why you have to use the standards you've built to determine the best opportunities, including who will be useful for you to collaborate with. Potential collaborators have to be resonant with where you've determined you're going and with how you're developing yourself out of higher levels of capability.

Your bigger commitments are going to require courage, and while you're going through a stage that requires courage, you'll want to be in relationships with people who are also committed and in a courage stage—people who are always growing.

Meeting your best standards, recognizing what will be useful for your growth and what won't be, is a huge part of being your best self and will help you to attract the right people.

Determining your future.

Who you'll be in the future comes from the growing power and impact of the filters and standards for evaluating, judging, and deciding what's acceptable to you and what isn't.

This is your confidence about how you're going to proceed into the future. And it's a confidence that few people have, which means that the best possible people will be attracted to how you're moving into the future because they want to do that themselves.

They can't come to you trying to sell something. The best people come to you and say, "I'd like to be part of how you're moving forward."

They can sense the energy, the learning, and the standards you have, and they want to cooperate with you. They want to, and have to, meet your standards, so you're not seeking anyone out—you're attracting.

And to meet your standards, they have to have been doing this themselves and to have independently and uniquely created something that would be of enormous value to you.

Part of being a person with standards who attracts others is being willing to turn away people who don't meet your standards. Keep in mind that there are 7.8 billion people on the planet, and you don't need them all.

Only for your best growth.

Many people struggle with trusting their own judgment. They aren't totally clear whether it's best to have complete faith in their own internal capabilities or to put all their trust in someone else's capabilities and judgments.

With a buyer mindset, this isn't a question you have to struggle with. The answer is that your current best judgments are absolutely reliable for choosing what your next best growth experiences can be—and this will always be the case going into the future.

Everybody lives their experience in relationship to what's available to them. You can maximize other people's experience, but you're always bouncing it off your own experience. You can learn from other people's standards, but you have a unique existence, and your experience isn't their experience.

Transformation, not status.

Nothing you've learned from your experience so far is setting you up to achieve a certain kind of set status in the future. Rather, everything you've learned is enabling you to be increasingly more transformative.

You're always looking for things that resonate with the direction you've determined is best for you, and this will include a lot of surprising new relationships, experiences, and opportunities.

But being a member of some sort of "club" is never the goal. Aiming for reaching a certain level or status isn't what's driving you.

Instead, it's all about growth and transformation.

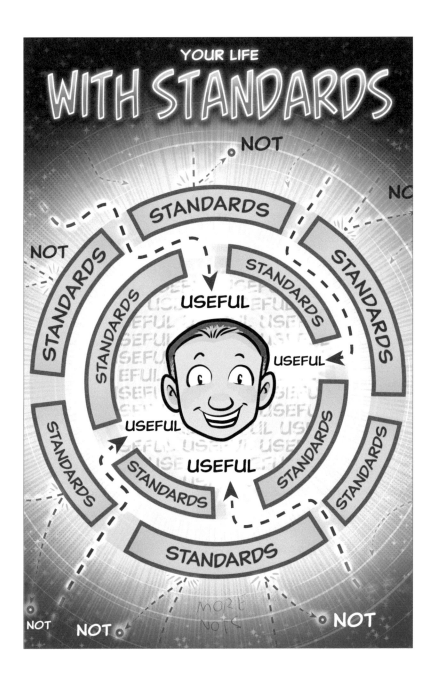

Chapter 5
Knowing What Doesn't Matter
You increasingly apply your growing standards to filter out and eliminate all those experiences that are not useful for your growth.

Simplifying and multiplying is a constant cycle.

Once you reach a certain level of growth, you have to simplify in order for new experiences to be of value.

You need to get back to what's crucial about you and your unique capabilities, and get down to the essence of what you've learned.

Once you're back to that simple state, all of a sudden, you can connect with all sorts of opportunities that can multiply your simplicity.

It isn't a straight line. You multiply, you reach a point where it gets complex and you have to simplify, and then you multiply out again. And the level at which you're simplifying and multiplying keeps progressing to a higher level, with greater knowledge of your unique capabilities and greater relationships and connections.

Lighten up, leave behind.
Every valuable lesson from your past energizes you, and everything from your past that has no further learning that you can get from it can now be discarded.

We can take a lesson in this from nature. Things in nature

are constantly discarding aspects of themselves that are no longer useful to them as they grow and thrive.

Similarly, we have to recognize what's useful for our future and what isn't, and be able to leave things behind.

Nothing pulling you back.
Your only important past experiences are ones that can deepen, expand, and multiply you forward.

If you find yourself entertaining something new that would be good for you to pursue, but you're still being tugged back by experiences from which you haven't learned the lessons, you need to go back and simplify those complicated experiences before you can move ahead.

Examining, extracting lessons from, and creating the meaning out of past experiences is also how we transform a negative experience into something positive and useful, and how we can move forward in our lives without being fearful of situations that remind us of negative experiences we've had.

You have to own the experience. You can't blame outside factors.

And it's just as important to get the right lesson out of experiences where you've gained something. For example, if you've been handed advantages in the past, it's the wrong lesson to think that in the future, people will just give you things you haven't earned. That's the kind lesson that can harm you.

Achievable and measurable.
You'll notice as you go forward that everything you want in your future has the qualities of being both more

achievable and more measurable than things you did in the past. Anything that doesn't have those two qualities is meaningless. If you can't achieve it and you can't measure it, it can't be the thing you're focusing on right now.

You won't be able to communicate a project effectively to the other people who need to be involved unless the project is achievable within a defined period of time and its success is clear-cut and measurable with either a number or an event.

The goals that excite you will increasingly meet these criteria, and that's a result of your constantly bringing forward lessons from your past experiences.

Having achievable and measurable goals will mean that your capability is constantly growing, and that's going to give you the confidence needed to commit to bigger and bigger projects.

Being your own best blueprint.

You'll find that your deepening, expanding, uniquely custom-designed rules for yourself are vastly more important and useful to you than anyone else's general instructions or advice.

General advice can be useful, and learning from someone else's experience can save you a lot of time, but in order for you to be really successful, it has to be your blueprint, not someone else's.

You have to have this mindset to be the buyer, because otherwise you're playing by someone else's terms. And you're never as good at playing by someone else's rules as they are.

Bigger, better, more useful.

Every new situation and circumstance you're in, you'll now size up on the basis of how and when it will contribute to your being a more creative, productive, and collaborative person in a bigger future.

A lot of people might know what they're best at and what they're willing to do, but it's also about knowing the other side of it, which is what you absolutely will not do. And that's a standard.

You have an unlimited number of future opportunities, which means there are an enormous number of them that you don't have to take.

I didn't know this fact ten years ago, and ten years ago, I might have taken many opportunities I wouldn't take today. But my experience has now taught me to stick within the confines of the rules and standards I've created and developed out of all my past experiences.

You know what you're good at, what you like doing, what you don't like doing, and what you're looking for. And what you're looking for most is other people who are unique at what they do. Someone else's uniqueness is completely different from yours, but if it's a right match, there's a collaborative resonance that happens. There's no competition with them because you're doing different things, but the way they're going about doing their thing supports the way you're going about doing your thing.

Chapter 6
Knowing Who Will Grow

You utilize the full strength of your growth standards to identify those individuals who are most committed to growing into your future.

You're creating a future, and you don't want to do it alone. We're social creatures. Everybody wants a community, and the kind of community you need is a transforming community.

Part of our growth is our own self-discovery, but a lot of it involves benefiting from the self-discovery and growth of others.

I'm very conscious of the fact that who I am and how I'm growing as an individual is one of the most powerful aspects of my coaching right now. There are always new concepts and tools that we teach at Strategic Coach, but people benefiting from my self-discovery and growth is also a factor.

And one of my standards is that I'm only looking to work with other people who are committed to self-discovery and growth.

Best growth standards.
Everyone who grows achieves their progress and improvement by transforming frustrating and painful failures into rules and measurements for satisfying success.

How someone reacts to failures can be a very strong indicator of where they are in terms of standards they've set for themselves.

If someone feels frustrated and stuck as a result of previous failures, they don't have a transformative mindset. They haven't learned how to transform their negative experiences into lessons that will help them avoid negative experiences in the future.

Someone with a transformative mindset isn't irked by negative experiences they've had in the past because they've taken the lesson from the experience.

Identifying who's who.

You'll be increasingly on the lookout for, and alert to, individuals whose thoughts, words, actions, and results clearly indicate that their constant motivation is to expand who they are.

That's the only thing I'm out to buy: other people who are transforming themselves.

All of us who do this are alike in that way, but the way each of us does it is totally different.

Still, it's like a radio beam that you'll pick up on. You gather knowledge all the time. You'll recognize a like-minded individual by the way they conduct themselves and the way they treat other people, and you'll know they're somebody who could be worth associating with.

You won't be distracted by non-transformative people. Your radar won't pick them up because you're not looking for them.

They grow, you grow.

In order to be constantly growing, you have to continually increase both the number and unique variety of other individuals who have come to the same conclusion about their own growth as you have.

My growth would be much slower if I weren't surrounded by other people who are growing. I'm spurred on by their growth. When they make a big jump, I don't want to fall behind them.

But this isn't about self-comparison. It's about inspiration. The growing I'm doing is ultimately for myself. I don't want to get cut off from the power and inspiration of other people's brains. Together, we're creating something that's bigger than all of us. And I want to keep up my part of that.

The larger your community of transformers, the more transformative people you surround yourself with, the easier it is to do extraordinary things.

We like things to be normal and to do normal things. And the more you associate with people who strive to do, and who *do*, extraordinary things, the more that doing extraordinary things becomes normal for you.

Strong getting stronger.
Your expanding understanding and appreciation of other individuals' ways of unique growth will strengthen your own confidence and excitement about what will always lie ahead of you. This is a dynamic, fluid process.

If you're playing this game, you can never say, "Okay, that's it. I've had enough growth." Because at that point, you're out of the game.

I've seen people do that, and it doesn't make them happy. They grow and grow, and then they stop growing. They had the notion that a certain amount of growth would get them somewhere specific, and once they get there, they discover it doesn't have any of the rewards that continually growing has.

What they weren't clear about is that what they really wanted was the growth.

When you're in the activity of growth, the thrill keeps going up. And it multiplies according to how many people are involved in it with you.

Always greater awareness.
This process of collaborative growth, which started with your own self-recognition, will never slow down or come to an end because your growing awareness of its rewards will always accelerate your enjoyment.

The activity is its own reward, and that's the best type of activity. But you can't be constantly doing it on your own. You'll need more and more support with more and more people.

A big part of what really excites us as humans, and what keeps us going and getting better as individuals, is being spurred on by the example of other people constantly spurring themselves on.

The number one thing that human beings buy is other people's examples of always growing because it reinforces their own growth.

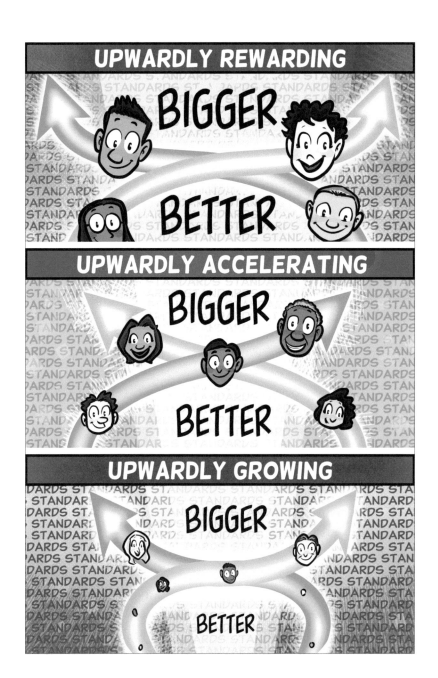

Chapter 7
Knowing What Growers Want

You are increasingly skilled at understanding what the best people in your future are striving for most in theirs.

In the best collaborations, the qualities you're looking for in the other person are the same ones they're looking for in you. What applies to you applies to them.

You can't sell them your experience; you can only provide them with the transformation of your experience into lessons, rules, and shortcuts. You each recognize that what the other has learned from their experience is valuable. You're both looking for a variety of transformative experience.

You aren't selling to each other. You're buying into each other.

Always becoming better.

You can always be meeting and connecting with an increasing number of uniquely talented and creative individuals who, like you, are always striving to become better in all areas of their lives.

You'll always be developing standards for all parts of your life, not just one area.

When a person has standards in only one area of their life, and that's the area they project outward, then what they're projecting outward doesn't represent their life. What you perceive about a person like that is misleading.

They're presenting an image that they have their act together, but it's only what they're presenting. Backstage, they don't have their act together at all, and they try to hide that because it conflicts with the image they're setting.

But it has to be consistent all the way through. Having standards has to be a consistent thing, 360 degrees.

You grow, they grow.
The magic formula for your future is simply to focus on your own growth. This alone will attract other growth-motivated individuals to connect with you.

You have to *be* what you want to attract. Otherwise, how would you know what to look for? And as you grow, you're going to inspire other people to grow.

When you see the people around you growing, you're pushed to make your own jumps because you don't want to get left behind.

And as you're focused on your own growth, it's going to inspire all the growth-minded people around you in the same way.

Collaborating with future best.
Every day, you're committed to and striving to grow into the "best future you." And it's that version of you that the best potential collaborators right now and in the future will most want to collaborate with.

So it's your goal, which you're open about having, that attracts the best individuals to collaborate with you, and it's those collaborations that will be of huge help to you in taking the next steps toward reaching that very goal.

The future you that you're working toward is a message you're sending out. It becomes a back-and-forth communication.

Sharing everyone's tested truths.

It's gratifying to be a contributor to a network of growth-committed individuals who, like you, are excited about sharing their proven breakthroughs in creating new kinds of creative, productive, and profitable value.

Each of you in the network can consider yourself in the value creation business because you're not only growing yourself, you're actually creating value through your growth. The value you have to offer in the marketplace is a byproduct of the growing you're always doing.

Something that you never want to do is to keep your growth mindset a secret. It's what's ultimately going to attract the best possible people for you to take on as collaborators, and it's what's going to lead you to attracting the best possible customers and clients.

There's no competition at all here. It's the opposite of how things are when everyone is competing for status, looking to one-up each other. You want to see others continue to grow, and they want the same for you, because everybody can benefit from everyone else sharing the benefits of their own growth.

Because you're always growing, you'll want to see everything around you grow. You'll notice non-growth, and you won't want that to be a part of what you do.

Combining what works best.

You'll be powerfully supported in your individual progress

and achievement by the multiplying combinations of other individuals' unique insights, innovations, and solutions. There is reciprocity among growing individuals who share the benefits of their growth.

I'm always working on myself, but the reason I'm doing that is to create greater value for the collaborative growth in Strategic Coach workshops. And then I learn things in the workshops that make me grow, and I go out by myself to test out how that growth works so I can take it back to the next workshop.

It's a closed loop, always moving from collaborative growth to individual growth, and then bringing something back at a higher level.

The general world doesn't support this, so the energy you need won't come from there. But in a group of like-minded individuals, the energy you need is being supported by other people's activities, so you don't have to provide all that energy just to support yourself at your current level of growth.

Now, all of that energy can be used toward creativity and innovation.

Chapter 8
Knowing Why They'll Stay

Your expanding network of transformative innovators is self-multiplying because once someone experiences how being in it makes everything bigger and better, there is never any reason to leave.

At this point, you've tested all sorts of arrangements in the world, made attempts to cooperate, and tried out being a seller, where you've had to change yourself to be agreeable to someone else.

But the more you build up your standards about what's useful to you and what isn't, the more you become the buyer of your next experiences. And since you're a transformative innovator and you want to multiply, whom you're multiplying with are other transformative innovators.

And guess what: because they've also been building up their standards, they're buying into you just as you're buying into them.

As long as you stick to your standards, they'll stay attracted because they're looking for standards that keep getting better. You won't lose them as long as you continue reinforcing what attracted them in the first place.

What they admire most about you is that you keep getting clearer and more consistent about the things you'll do and the things you won't do. It goes both ways. It's the mutual attraction of self-organizing collaborators.

Clarifying powerful aspirations.

Your own daily example of transforming yourself becomes a greater force that encourages every other innovative transformer in your network to increase their own ambitions to do the same.

Even if you're totally clear about how you can transform yourself, you want reinforcement for that. And you get that reinforcement in a network of people who are all trying to transform and grow, and who are all watching and learning from one another.

The only thing you need in order to stay a member of a network of transformative people is to always reinforce your own standards, getting clearer and clearer on them, becoming a better and better buyer.

Multiplying best innovators.

The greatest capability outside of yourself that most supports and propels your daily growth is the multiplication of the best innovators who are enthusiastically transforming themselves in your network.

We can only be the center of our own universe, so you might think of it as *your* network, but it's their network too. And you're a part of it.

Every person in the network is working on their own growth, and that's the electricity that keeps it all running. You have to contribute to the energy supply to get access to the energy supply.

The community is essential. You can't always be the buyer

unless you're in a community of people who share your buyer mindset.

Greater clarity, confidence, and capability.

Your enthusiasm and sense of momentum about your transformative network continually grows because you can see that all of the new growth-minded innovators you're attracting automatically reinforce the overall clarity, confidence, and capability of everyone else in the community.

It's the opposite of being a seller, where everyone you see is a potential competitor for rewards that seem in scarce supply. When you're in the selling game, nobody is an ally.

But when you're a member of a community of buyers, everyone working on themselves is assisting everyone else working on themselves.

Going from having a seller mindset to a buyer mindset is like suddenly being able to see an abundance of rewards and all the opportunities that are out there, where before there was scarcity.

Excitement of breaking through.

You know from your own experience of moving from being a seller to a buyer that every innovator who joins your network will be permanently committed to staying inside it because of this first and lasting experience of breaking through into a future that keeps getting bigger and better.

It's binary. When you cross over, it's all the way. It's going completely from allowing the power for your growth to lie outside of yourself to deciding that the power is always going to be inside of yourself, to be based on your standards of what's useful and what isn't.

The crossing over can only happen as the result of the decision, the goal, and the commitment on the part of the individual themselves. You can't make the move for someone else. They have to want it, and once someone wants it, it's all out there for them.

Once you make the decision to stop twisting yourself out of shape trying to be a seller and join this buyer universe, you won't want to leave.

You'll notice as soon as you walk away from a check because you know it won't be a positive creative experience, that the missed opportunity will soon be filled up with a much better opportunity. This is because as soon as you've made the change, you'll start showing up on the radars of other individuals who have made the same change for themselves.

Growth motivating growth.

The experience of always growing greater personal capability and confidence in unpredictably new ways is permanently motivating, and knowing that this is true for you, you also know that it's true for all the other growth-minded innovators who are joining you.

You've probably had experience in this type of relationship, where you just love getting together with the person, and your mind always expands when you're with them. Now you have the context for looking at what's going on in that type of relationship. And if it was in the margins of your life, you're now deciding to make it the center and to always be expanding that center outward.

BEST PEOPLE TRANSFORMING

Conclusion
Buyers Multiplying More Buyers
You increasingly transform the most powerful aspirations of your best people into greater clarity, confidence, and capability for them — which in turn multiplies your own best aspirations.

When you're constantly simplifying yourself with the clarity of your standards, this allows you to multiply yourself with other people who also have standards.

Most people sell themselves as the first step of selling. The first buying you do is buying yourself as the center of everything, and every further step has to be a reinforcement of your own uniqueness and your own unique capabilities.

Clearest, most confident vision.
Increasingly owning your transformed experiences provides you with a growing wisdom to provide equally proprietary vision and focus to every like-minded achiever who joins your expanding network of superior resources and capabilities.

What you grant to yourself, you also grant to other people, and this includes ownership of one's experiences. You can't be who you want to be unless you grant that to everybody around you.

Some people don't want ownership of their own experiences, and those people won't be part of your network. As your experience ownership increases, more and more, you're going to notice people who are doing the same. Increasingly, you'll only see the people who are operating at your level.

There's no comparison there. Instead, there's resonance. You're all equally powerful, and you all know that you can learn from one another without compromising who you are as individuals.

The best are transforming themselves.

You don't have to convince, sell, or persuade anyone else to emulate how you're transforming yourself into a bigger and better future, because the best people will be attracted to your observable direction, energy, and movement, and they'll be inspired to apply your example to their own growth opportunities.

We live in a great time in that most of us are allowed to be ourselves, but at the same time, there's a lot of temptation out there to imitate others.

But the people who will join your network won't just be trying to imitate you; they'll be making the decision to take the same approach to themselves as you have to yourself.

You're inspiring them. There's no manipulation or convincing for you to do. You'll inspire simply through your commitment to being clear about your standards and to always being the buyer.

Increased daily motivation.

Always being the buyer is going to continually increase your daily clarity, confidence, and capability to create the best new methods, strategies, and opportunities for everyone in the world whose ambitions and success most support your own.

In this way, you're not just doing it for yourself. You're also creating value for other people who have decided for themselves to follow the same path.

When you've explored something for yourself, and you know that there are other people who'd like to further the mapping of the territory, you'll want to share it with them. It's natural for humans that when we're confronted with an obstacle outside of ourselves, we share everything we know about getting around the obstacle.

The obstacle out in the world is the temptation to not be who you are, and so you share how you go about being yourself with others who have also chosen to be who they are.

Doing it yourself first is what heightens the possibility of a community of like-minded people forming around you. You want the community, but you don't get it until you first prove to yourself that you can go it alone.

Then once you have the community, you'll get better every day at being the buyer and helping others to do the same.

Unified growing momentum.

Everyone's growing sense of breaking through their next barriers, restrictions, limitations, and obstacles is what unifies everyone's growing momentum.

The most persuasive sign that something's good for you is that you can feel momentum—both personal momentum and from being part of something bigger that has momentum to it.

This momentum frees up your mind from telling you that

you have to be doing things you don't like doing. You can focus just on the activities you're doing that you like and that are best for you, and the collective momentum carries you and everyone else forward.

When you first start, you're self-powered, having to lift yourself up, but there's a bigger, faster power supporting you now. And all the people who are sharing in the collective momentum are the ones that are creating the momentum.

The buying decision.
Life is either buying or selling. It's your choice. The world trains us to be sellers. Only you can train yourself to be the buyer.

If the growth of your success in the world always starts outside of yourself, with what other people are doing, you'll always be the seller. But if the growth of your success in the world always starts inside of yourself, you'll always be the buyer.

Many people look outside of themselves for the answer to the question of who they are, but the issue isn't really a question and answer—it's a decision.

The decision is that you're going to become the master of your own life. And you'll find that the more you take responsibility for the uniqueness of your own life, everything you hoped to find by selling will be attracted to you. You don't have to sell it.

You'll meet and link up with everybody else who's made the choice to train themselves to be the buyer.

The Strategic Coach Program
For Ambitious, Collaborative Entrepreneurs

You commit to growing upward through three transformative levels, giving yourself 25 years to exponentially improve every aspect of your work and life.

"Always be the buyer" is a crucial capability and a natural result of everything we coach in The Strategic Coach Program, a quarterly workshop experience for successful entrepreneurs who are committed and devoted to business and industry transformation for the long-term, for 25 years and beyond.

The Program has a destination for all participants—creating more and more of what we call "Free Zone Frontiers." This means taking advantage of your own unique capabilities, the unique capabilities around you, your unique opportunities, and your unique circumstances, and putting the emphasis on creating a life that is free of competition.

Most entrepreneurs grow up in a system where they think competition is the name of the game. The general way of looking at the world is that the natural state of affairs is competition, and collaboration is an anomaly.

Free Zone Frontier

The Free Zone Frontier is a whole new level of entrepreneurship that many people don't even know is possible. But once you start putting the framework in place, new possibilities open up for you. You create zones that are purely about collaboration. You start recognizing that collaboration is the natural state, and competition is the anomaly. It makes you look at things totally differently.

Strategic Coach has continually created concepts and thinking tools that allow entrepreneurs to more and more see their future in terms of Free Zones that have no competition.

Three levels of entrepreneurial growth.

Strategic Coach participants continually transform how they think, make decisions, communicate, and take action based on their use of dozens of unique entrepreneurial mindsets we've developed. The Program has been refined through decades of entrepreneurial testing and is the most concentrated, massive discovery process in the world created solely for transformative entrepreneurs who want to create new Free Zones.

Over the years, we've observed that our clients' development happens in levels of mastery. And so, we've organized the Program into three levels of participation, each of which involves two different types of transformation:

The Signature Level. The first level is devoted to your *personal* transformation, which has to do with how you're spending your time as an entrepreneur as well as how you're taking advantage of your personal freedom outside of business that your entrepreneurial success affords you. Focusing on improving yourself on a personal level before you move on to making significant changes in other aspects of your life and business is key because you have to simplify before you can multiply.

The second aspect of the Signature Level is how you look at your *teamwork*. This means seeing that your future consists of teamwork with others whose unique capabilities complement your own, leading to bigger and better goals that constantly get achieved at a measurably higher rate.

The 10x Ambition Level. Once you feel confident about your own personal transformation and have access to ever-expanding teamwork, you can think much bigger in terms of your *company*. An idea that at one time would have seemed scary and even impossible—growing your business 10x—is no longer a wild dream but a result of the systematic expansion of the teamwork model you've established. And because you're stable in the center, you won't get thrown off balance by exponential growth. Your life stays balanced and integrated even as things grow around you.

And that's when you're in a position to transform your relationship with your *market*. This is when your company has a huge impact on the marketplace that competitors can't even understand because they're not going through this transformative structure or thinking in terms of 25 years as you are. Thinking in terms of 25 years gives you an expansive sense of freedom and the ability to have big picture goals.

The Free Zone Frontier Level. Once you've mastered the first four areas of transformation, you're at the point where your company is self-managing and self-multiplying, which means that your time can now be totally freed up. At this stage, competitors become collaborators and it becomes all about your *industry*. You can consider everything you've created as a single capability you can now match up with another company's to create collaborations that go way beyond 10x.

And, finally, it becomes *global*. You immediately see that there are possibilities of going global—it's just a matter of combining your capabilities with those of others to create something exponentially bigger than you could ever have achieved on your own.

Global collaborative community.

Entrepreneurism can be a lonely activity. You have goals that the people you grew up with don't understand. Your family might not comprehend you at all and don't know why you keep wanting to expand, why you want to take new risks, why you want to jump to the next level. And so it becomes proportionately more important as you gain your own individual mastery that you're in a community of thousands of individuals who are on exactly the same journey.

In The Strategic Coach Program, you benefit from not only your own continual individual mastery but from the constant expansion of support from and collaboration with a growing global community of extraordinarily liberated entrepreneurs who will increasingly share with you their deep wisdom and creative breakthroughs as innovators in hundreds of different industries and markets.

If you've reached a jumping off point in your entrepreneurial career where you're beyond ready to multiply all of your capabilities and opportunities into a 10x more creative and productive formula that keeps getting simpler and more satisfying, we're ready for you.

For more information and to register for The Strategic Coach Program, call 416.531.7399 or 1.800.387.3206, or visit us online at *strategiccoach.com*.

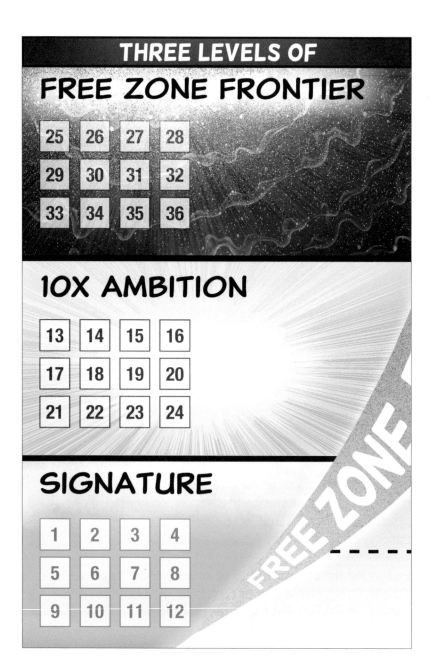

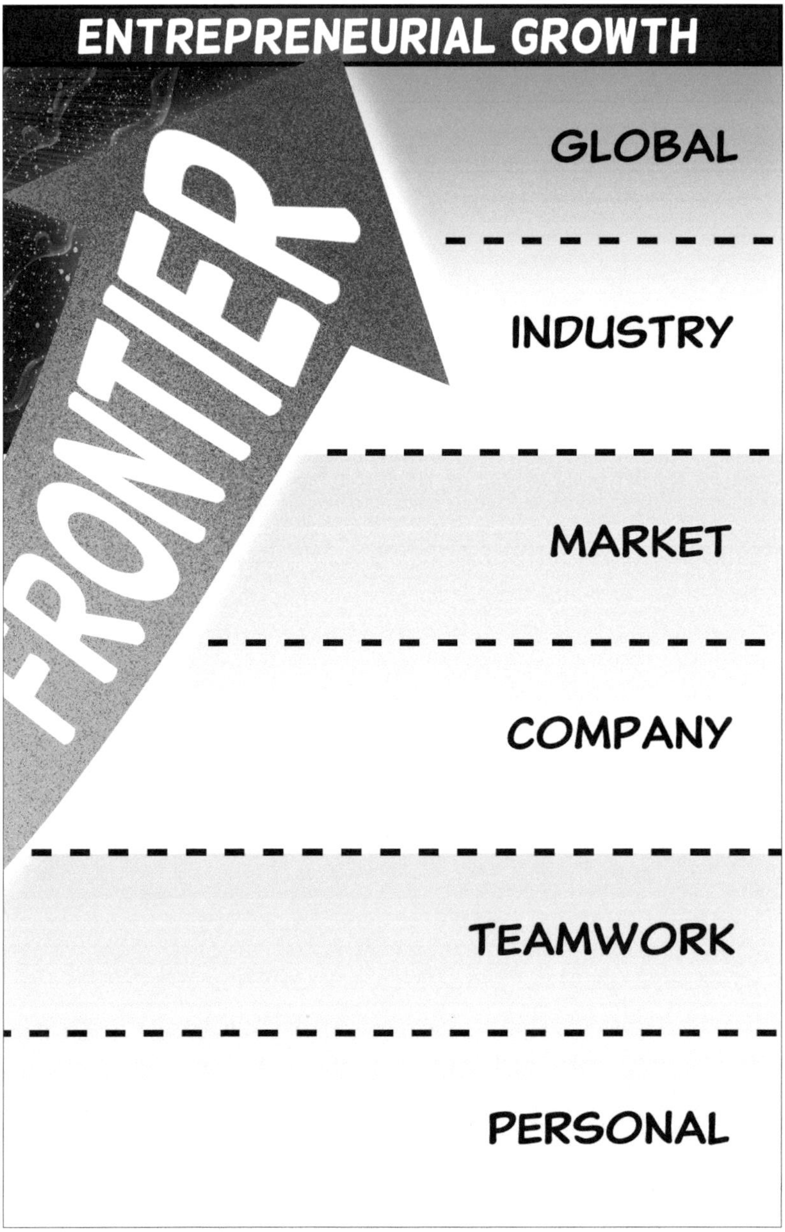

ENTREPRENEURIAL GROWTH

FRONTIER

GLOBAL

INDUSTRY

MARKET

COMPANY

TEAMWORK

PERSONAL

Always Be The Buyer Scorecard

Turn the page to view the Mindset Scorecard and read through the four statements for each mindset. Give yourself a score of 1 to 12 based on where your own mindset falls on the spectrum. Put each mindset's score in the first column at the right, and then add up all eight and put the total at the bottom.

Then, think about what scores would represent progress for you over the next quarter. Write these in the second scoring column, add them up, and write in the total.

When you compare the two scores, you can see where you want to go in terms of your achievements and ambitions.

Mindsets	1	2	3	4	5	6
1 Knowing Who You'll Always Be	You've never had any feeling that you're worth anything in yourself, and as a result, you don't think that anyone else values who you are.			You're tired of trying to pretend that you're someone you're not, and you're ready to start being more of who you actually are.		
2 Knowing Where You're Going	You're confused about where things are going, feeling anxious and pessimistic that others are always changing the game.			You're increasingly dissatisfied and bored with "groupthink" rules and predictions, wanting now to build your own internal rules.		
3 Knowing What You're Leaving	You've spent most of your life trapped in long-ago emotions and memories that prevent you from living confidently in the present.			You realize that everything you've experimented with so far is now over, and you want to transform your present into a bigger future.		
4 Knowing What Matters Most	You've never developed any personal wisdom or strategy about which ongoing experiences are good or bad for your future.			You've reached your lifetime quota for being rejected as a seller. Now you want to establish the rules of who gets to sell to you.		
5 Knowing What Doesn't Matter	Your life has continually been sidetracked and undermined by investing your time in unrealistic and wasteful activities.			You've decided that you've had enough failure and dissatisfaction at this point to now begin learning everything that will lead to success.		
6 Knowing Who Will Grow	Your own lack of self-awareness and self-knowledge prevents you from identifying other people who might be good for your future.			You are now tired of relating to other people based on what you're missing. From now on, it will be based on who you can grow with.		
7 Knowing What Growers Want	You are so trapped in your own worst fears and anxieties that you think everyone else also has negative obsessions about you.			You keep being painfully reminded that it's a mistake to assume what others want, so now you are committed to discovering the truth.		
8 Knowing Why They'll Stay	You never worked or lived with anyone who had any ambition except to stay where they are, which is all that you've ever done.			You're just realizing that to always be growing, you have to surround yourself from now on only with others who are always growing.		
Scorecard	➡	➡	➡	➡	➡	➡

7	8	9	10	11	12	Score Now	Score Next
You always make sure to use the best proven presentation strategies to impress those with the most power and money to help you.			You derive maximum value from your best and worst experiences to determine who you always are when you're at your best.				
You've always joined the "in groups" throughout your life that make it seem that you're "in the know" even when you're not.			You continually clarify your best possible future with measurable goals that represent the best growth of your best capabilities.				
You're now holding onto and defending a business and social status that you worked very hard to achieve. Nothing new interests you.			You increasingly transform your daily experience going forward to eliminate everything that doesn't support who you're growing into.				
What matters most to you is winning the ongoing business of those buyers who automatically boost your future reputation.			You create powerful filters of high personal standards by which you determine which ongoing experiences are best for growth.				
You planned from the beginning of your personal and work life to pattern everything you do on others who are most admired.			You increasingly apply your growing standards to filter out and eliminate all those experiences that are not useful for your growth.				
You have continually formed your best relationships based on your most important goals for increasing your own status and reputation.			You utilize the full strength of your growth standards to identify those individuals who are most committed to growing into your future.				
Your entire success going forward is based on the belief that everyone wants what you want but isn't as good as you are at achieving it.			You are increasingly skilled at understanding what the best people in your future are striving for most in theirs.				
Your whole life has been about achieving and maintaining your status of always meeting other people's standards of success.			Your expanding network of transformative innovators is self-multiplying because there is never any reason to leave.				
➡	➡	➡	➡	➡	➡		

About The Author
Dan Sullivan

Dan Sullivan is the founder and president of The Strategic Coach Inc. and creator of The Strategic Coach® Program, which helps accomplished entrepreneurs reach new heights of success and happiness. He has over 40 years of experience as a strategic planner and coach to entrepreneurial individuals and groups. He is author of over 30 publications, including *The 80% Approach*™, *The Dan Sullivan Question*, *Ambition Scorecard*, *Wanting What You Want*, *The 4 C's Formula*, *The 25-Year Framework*, *The Game Changer*, *The 10x Mind Expander*, *The Mindset Scorecard*, *The Self-Managing Company*, *Procrastination Priority*, *The Gap And The Gain*, *The ABC Breakthrough*, *Extraordinary Impact Filter*, *Capableism*, *My Plan For Living To 156*, *WhoNotHow*, *Your Life As A Strategy Circle*, *Who Do You Want To Be A Hero To?*, and *Free Zone Frontier*, and is co-author with Catherine Nomura of *The Laws of Lifetime Growth*.

Made in United States
Troutdale, OR
01/05/2024

16714988R00050